Marketing Trends

SUPERCYCLES

by Donald R. Libey

Edited By Catherine Eberlein
Potentials In Marketing Magazine

**Ten Major
Trends For
The Rebirth
Of Marketing
In The New
Century**

QUANTITY SALES

Most Lakewood books are available at special quantity discounts when purchased in bulk by companies, organizations and special-interest groups. Custom imprinting or excerpting can also be done to fit special needs. For details write: Lakewood Books, 50 South Ninth Street, Minneapolis, MN 55402 or call 612/333-0471.

■ ■ ■

LAKEWOOD BOOKS
50 South Ninth Street
Minneapolis, MN 55402
612/333-0471

Publisher: Mary G. Hanson
Editor: Catherine Eberlein
Production Manager: Pat Grawert
Production Editor: Susan Abbott
Designer: Sandra Saima

10 9 8 7 6 5 4 3 2 1

Lakewood Publications, Inc., is a subsidiary of Maclean Hunter Publishing Company. Lakewood publishes *Potentials In Marketing* Magazine and its annual High Performance Marketing Conference; *TRAINING Magazine, The Human Side of Business; The Training Directors' Forum Newsletter; Creative Training Techniques Newsletter; The Service Edge Newsletter; Total Quality Newsletter; Recreation Resources Magazine,* and other business periodicals, books and conferences.

Donald R. Libey
The Libey Consultancy Incorporated
1308 Keswick Avenue
Haddon Heights, NJ 08035; 609/573-9448

ISBN 0-943210-25-9

TABLE OF CONTENTS

FOREWORD

THE REBIRTH OF MARKETING

The age of customer focus.

These are heady times. We stand at the threshold of the new century and a new millennium, a unique event that will not be repeated in our lifetimes. In fact, what we will experience happens only once every 100 years and once every 1,000 years.

These are also dangerous times. The engines of change are running at full throttle; danger and opportunity have never been more competitive. The thin edge of the economic razor has never been sharper, nor has it ever cut those who stumble so deep.

These times offer, however, a rare opportunity for the strategically enlightened marketer. The decisions you make today are the decisions that will shape your company's future in the new century.

Historically the decade before the turn of the century is rife with change, pregnant with progress and electric with freneticism. Until now, our lives have been historically measured by *where we have come from*; soon we must futuristically measure our lives by *where we are going*.

Businesses, like living things, have life cycles: they wax and wane, ebb and flow, bloom and decay. And so it is with marketing. All around us the industry is transforming, *becoming* something newer and larger that resembles nothing in our experience. Marketing as we have known it is disappearing and a new order of business has been born. The *velocity* of change is staggering. The *frequency* and *amplitude* of change are narrowing and increasing exponentially. The luxury of time and space no longer exist.

The "old school" marketing industry has entered the inevitable phase of *freneticism* and the evidence of this energy is clear. There are insatiable demands for profits; intolerance of expansion investment; a shift from marketing-driven to finance-driven operating policies; intense politicization of management. Automation is used as a respite from labor-intensiveness; there is margin erosion; distrust and abandonment of the old formulas and conventions; competitive homogeneity; and migration from exhausted U.S. markets to developing international markets.

How do we create order out of chaos?

FOCUS ON THE CUSTOMER

As we move into the new century and the new millennium, those of us who survive the rebirth of marketing will do so because of our total, compulsive focus on the individual customer. At every level of marketing, the immediate and all-consuming focus of success will be at the next commercial level of customers.

This new order of customer-focused marketing will evoke rational and logical trends in marketing. Each of these emergent trends will be controversial, provocative and initially be denied as being impossible, impractical and improbable.

11

These new trends, however, will come to dominate marketing in the same way that every new standard of marketing progress has come to dominate the industry over the preceding four decades.

To create order out of chaos we must focus on the relevance of what it is that we do. Ours is not a new social experiment or the creation of a new world order. What we do — now and in the future — is to create *trade*.

We stimulate the fundamental process of buying and selling. And the prime purpose of commerce is profit. We need to master the skills and proprieties of creating profit because it has the capacity for good for the greatest number of people.

And so, we need to begin the necessary dialogue for the strategic rebirth of marketing in the new century: *Customer-Focused Marketing*. There are 10 "Supercycles" or macro concepts that compose customer-focused marketing, and within each there are micro concepts (subcycles and microcycles) that will inevitably pertain. Here's how I define these concepts:

■ A **SUPERCYCLE** represents something that society has already decided and comes to expect as a constant of commerce. For example, *quality* has been elevated to the level of supercycle in recent years and has been responsible for the birth of an entire industry. Once the vision of a supercycle concept has been elevated to this point, it can't be taken away from customers.

■ A **SUBCYCLE** is something specific that your industry can do to create and service customers relative to the supercycle.

■ A **MICROCYCLE** is a competitive strategy that your individual company can apply as a response to the subcycle.

As this book takes you through each of the ten supercycles — the major trends for the rebirth of marketing in the new century — use it as a means to better define your own company's strategies to totally and compulsively focus on your individual customers.

Donald R. Libey
September 1993

SUPERCYCLE ONE:

CUSTOMER-FOCUSED TIME

*Marketers who reduce time from trade relationships
will invest in a competitive corporate future*

The perceptual understanding of time has changed subtly yet totally. We have stopped thinking of time in blocks of years, months or days, and now view it in blocks of hours, minutes, seconds and now nanoseconds. Time, as it relates to trade, has been inexorably changed and compressed.

Instantaneity, as a necessary competitive enhancement to trade, will demand a total overhaul of the philosophic, technical and management foundations now in place in American business. Instantaneity, as a trade-shaping, customer expectation will place enormous strategic planning and financial burdens upon marketing organizations that can't be recouped under existing return on investment philosophies.

The current obsession with quarterly earnings in an industry managed by finance managers rather than by marketers must give way to an obsession with customer acquisition and retention if that industry is to survive. While financial stability is a necessary and positive thing, the planning and strategic direction of an industry is a job for visionaries, not accountants. In short, "There are some things that are so important, you can't afford to know what they cost." (Larry Quadracci, president of Quad/Graphics.)

CUSTOMER-FOCUSED TIME IS MORE THAN A CONCEPT

Customer-focused time is the *sine qua non* of strategic futurism. Every commercial trade endeavor going forward will have at its foundation time-dominated and time-denominated goals and objectives. A marketer who begins today to reduce every vestige of time from the trade relationship and process will be investing in a competitive corporate future.

The term *customer-focused* necessitates a total, paradigmatic shift. When the lid is peeled off most marketing organizations today, there is precious little that goes on that is customer-focused. The focus is on survival and all time expands to serve the body of the business, not the customers.

The clear symptom of a diseased company is the amount of time squandered on endless meetings where the customer is not even remotely considered. Management of these dying companies is almost always a central elite management. The only contact with customers or their expectations is through an osmotic process that filters out any possibility of contracting a dose of reality.

The CEOs of such "old school" marketing companies have long ago abdicated their primary role as customer advocate. They have adopted the mantle of isolationism and have buried their vision in the minutia of internal management.

The paradigmatic shift to a true customer focus is a monumental undertaking. Literally every action, decision and move the company makes must be made with the focus on the customer, and then with a strategic focus on time. Access by the customer must be instantaneous and in the form the customer specifies. Ordering must be instantaneous and all-encompassing — one-stop, complete, no follow-up required — and all in real time.

■ ■ ■

Technology equals time;
it creates the state of
instantaneity.

Distribution must be instantaneous and universal. Fulfillment, as a business function, will undergo massive changes in the years ahead. The focus will be on moving goods to customers within hours and not on the internal paperwork and processes necessary to orderly fulfillment. Computerization, automation and geographic decentralization will attain levels of development and sophistication as yet unconceived.

Some will argue that the essential processes of business can't simply be time-eliminated in absolute favor of customer-focused time; chaos will reign and corporate efficiency will suffer. That is, of course, true. Yet there is no advocacy for doing harm to the stability of business functions.

The essential business functions should be as tight and as efficient as they now are in our present business process-focused environment. The gain in time will not be made by throwing out the business controls, it will be made by the ascendancy of technology. Technology equals time; it creates the state of instantaneity.

SUBCYCLE: TIME-BASED MARKETING

The genesis of time-based marketing can be traced to the advent of 800 toll-free ordering numbers. The true motivation behind its popularity was not that the call was free, but in the fact that several days were saved in the process of receiving the products. The 800 number catered to the "I want it now" syndrome that would evolve and dominate the motivational aspects of marketing in the last 25 years of the 20th century.

Time-based marketing has emerged as the response to the customer's need for instant gratification. Whether business-to-business or consumer, a product that is identical in every respect to another will be perceived as competitively superior when it can be obtained immediately.

The first phase of time-based marketing was accomplished by Fred Smith, the founder of Federal Express, who altered the concept of *time*. The second phase evolved through Federal Express' extraordinary marketing vision. In partnership with marketers, Federal Express created a customer expectation of overnight delivery as a positive attribute. As more marketers embrace the power of the Federal Express appeal, this trend will not mature until total time-differentiation is the standard and norm for all product offerings.

The third phase of time-based marketing will be shared service and strategic distribution. In this phase, distribution systems will evolve into massive, integrated, shared service fulfillment centers that service multiple marketers.

Today's warehouse and shipping component servicing the end customer will alter dramatically. Its function will be the servicing of a network of contract fulfillment operations strategically located to provide eight hour delivery to any customer. Fulfillment will become layered as a result of the demand for time-based, customer-focused delivery.

It's important to remember that customer-focused time is an evolution, a force of industry organization. The massive power of such shifts can't be invoked by individual companies. Only through industry-wide integration will these systems emerge and strengthen the discipline of marketing. An individual company's response to time-based marketing is strategically defined as a *microcycle*.

MICROCYCLE: SAME-DAY DELIVERY

Think for a moment about your products and imagine all of the things you would have to do in order to put them into your customers' hands within the next eight hours. Each of those changes, tasks and goals will define the microcycle of same-day delivery as it relates to your specific company.

Second, think of all of your competitors and imagine what your particular specialty will be like when all of you are offering eight-hour delivery on essentially the same type of products. This vision is the logical outcome of the microcycle you will face in the new century.

Arriving at the point of dominion over this microcycle will require strategic planning in numerous components of your existing business. The personnel component will require attention, the financing component will have to be provided, the technology component will be a massive undertaking, the fulfillment systems component will be unlike anything existing at the moment.

Each functional area will demand redesign, redirection and reconstitution. And all of this will have to be done with the primary focus on customer-focused time and time-based marketing.

Ours is an increasingly competitive and complex business environment. Given the magnitude, amplitude and speed of change it isn't going to get any easier. If there is one absolute that you can count on as common sense fact, it is this: "The Customer is the wellspring of all business activity; in the beginning there was the customer."

■ ■ ■

SUPERCYCLE SUMMARY

■ **Customer-Focused Time:** The first of ten supercycles for the new century. It is defined as "all time shrinks in the perception of the customer and as a consequence, all marketing responses must shrink in time."

■ **Time-Based Marketing:** A subcycle of customer-focused time, which is defined as something specific that your industry can do to create and service customers relative to time.

■ **Same-Day Delivery:** A microcycle of time-based marketing. It is defined as a competitive strategy that your individual company can apply as a response to time-based marketing.

SUPERCYCLE TWO:

KNOWLEDGE-BASED MARKETING

The strategic application of knowledge-based marketing will forever alter the marketing industry.

Knowledge is power. And in the new century, your ability to provide knowledge to your customers will be the deciding factor in whether your company thrives or dies.

Customers have an insatiable need for information in a world that has become time-starved and exceedingly complex. There isn't enough time available to learn everything they must know in order to simply keep up with the chaotic realities of business. As customers increasingly demand greater amounts of more in-depth knowledge, your company's ability and capacity to provide that knowledge will be just as important as your ability and capacity to provide products. If your company can't provide the knowledge, your customers will go to those who can.

Marketers with an eye on the future must become expert in "Intellectual Commerce" — the merger of marketing and publishing — to leverage this insatiable need for knowledge and to keep customers coming back. By positioning their companies as the predominant research center and library of information for the industry into which they sell, and combining it with the best in service and fulfillment, these marketers will gain dominance in the marketplace.

A PREVIEW OF INTELLECTUAL COMMERCE

The way we currently inform, motivate and sell to customers will appear crude when compared with the advances to come. The publishing of information, as a process, is likely to be a hybrid of print, computer, telephone, fax and television to meet the customer's need for instantaneous information.

Customers will be able to select from an information menu that is relevant and based on their individual interests.

■■■

If your company can't provide knowledge, your customers will go to those who can.

For example, catalogs will become reference works that also sell products; customer service access will exist to inform, rather than to just solve errors. A business selling seeds will first be in the business of creating knowledgeable gardeners. The textbooks the company provides for its customers will instruct them about which seeds to buy and when, which is a massive paradigmatic shift. Today, seed companies prospect to gardeners; in the new century, they will prospect — and provide knowledge to — individuals who want to become gardeners.

Intellectual commerce in the business-to-business arena will provide education and knowledge to customers that is designed to enhance their competitiveness. Marketers will offer their business buyers useful information on how to integrate technology, meet increasing levels of compliance legislation and regulation, as well as provide specific training.

For example, a marketer of safety products for manufacturing companies will center his marketing efforts around providing comprehensive information on safety education and technical knowledge. If the company sells fire extinguishers, it will develop complete knowledge and reference databanks about fire prevention and training in the manufacturing environment. Ultimately, the company will evolve into a safety consulting firm for its customers, offering both goods and knowledge-based services.

SUBCYCLE: KNOWLEDGE-BASED MARKETING

The evolutionary organization of customer focused knowledge is a complex, expensive and necessary step into the future. The marketing and overt differentiation of knowledge will require that investment be shifted from the preoccupation with short-term returns to long-term dominance. And the level of investment in these systems will set apart the winners from the losers.

For example, elaborate systems will be developed, either internally or on an outside contract basis, to generate the quantity and quality of information necessary to meet the customer's demand for knowledge. This information will provide competitive, advantageous applications of goods and services.

Knowledge data banks will be used to augment and complement marketing data banks. Instantaneous, on-line research access will allow companies to answer customer demands for information about technical aspects of their ever-changing business component.

These types of knowledge-based systems will require new approaches to staffing. Support for research, writing, programming, publishing and education will be an integral requirement of marketers in the future. It's even conceivable that companies will develop separate departments to deliver a full range of research and publishing services aimed specifically at customers. Such departments will have responsibility for developing knowledge-based services that serve as primary customer acquisition magnets — and primary customer retention anchors.

THE CHANGING ROLE OF DATABASES

The marketing database systems now in vogue in the '90s will cease to be the be-all, end-all strategy for acquiring and retaining customers. In short order, the database will have no purpose other than being used as the means of delivering knowledge and information that will attract and retain customers.

As a result, the all-purpose database of the '90s will subdivide into multiple databases. Today, the database is virtually single-purposed; in the future it will be divided first into a marketing database and second, a knowledge database. Each of these new databases then further subdivide.

The marketing database will divide into product propensity and mailing databases, while the knowledge database will divide into research and compliance databases. Each of these sub-databases will further divide to create even more specific knowledge products.

The use of artificial intelligence will be critical to the process of organizing such massive and varied amounts of hyperknowledge in critical time and purpose frames. And it will be applied within broad objective parameters to learn from the living data, to apply governing parameters and to alter strategic direction.

For the first time, we will have the technological accessories that will allow us to expand past the human brain's paltry 10 percent capacity to govern 1000 percent more knowledge, and to still comprehend its meaning.

MICROCYCLE: KNOWLEDGE-BASED MARKETING PUBLISHING

The strategic application of knowledge-based marketing has the potential to alter forever the form, content, style and perception of the marketing industry. By adding knowledge, marketing will benefit from the addition of value.

The prime directive for this advancement will be the individual customer. Through the value-added application of knowledge, marketing will focus on the individual's specific wants, desires and business application needs. This is a far cry from the mass marketing appeals that dominated the marketing discipline during the last quarter of the 20th century.

By necessity, this process demands the development of knowledge systems that reach a minimum of two layers deep into the marketplace. This means that marketers will need to focus on the knowledge of the individual, within an individual business, within an individual business niche.

In effect, the marketer of the new century will assume the role of sub-industry publisher and disseminator of relevant knowledge. The staggering success and popularity of existing behemoths of knowledge — such as CompuServe, Prodigy and other interactive libraries of knowledge — point dramatically to this paradigmatic direction.

Clearly, those businesses that adopt publishing strategies to distribute knowledge will gain dominance over individual segments of the vast marketplace. Super-corporations that mount massive knowledge-based strategies to conglomerate marketplaces will extend their reach and multi-layered penetration. And, as advanced trading nations extend these strategies over entire geographic and demographic blocs, they will achieve primacy within the global economy and commercial milieu.

Libey Publishing Incorporated, our Washington, D.C.–based book publishing company, works with catalog companies and marketing-intensive corporations to develop and publish full-length, turnkey, proprietary books specific to the industry, products, and services of those companies. The books are sold to business and consumer customers through the catalogs and, as a result , the corporations achieve significant authority positioning in the minds of customers. As an example, if the Eagle Fire Safety Company sells fire equipment, the book is titled *The Eagle Guide to Commercial Fire Prevention and Safety.* The high-quality book written by an industry expert weaves in Eagle's products and describes their effective use in a comprehensive fire prevention program within the manufacturing and commercial setting. Eagle *sells* the books that *sell* its products. Pure genius.

In the final analysis, knowledge is power. And power is money.

■ ■ ■

SUPERCYCLE SUMMARY

▋ **Customer Focused Knowledge:** The second of ten supercycles for the new century. It is defined as: "Customers have an insatiable need for knowledge. The acquisition of this knowledge must be assured, instantaneous and comprehensive."

▋ **Knowledge-Based Marketing:** A subcycle of customer-focused knowledge which is defined as something specific your industry can do to provide customers with instant, complete information.

▋ **Knowledge-Based Marketing Publishing:** A microcycle of customer-focused knowledge. It is defined as a competitive strategy that your individual company can apply as a response to customer-focused knowledge.

SUPERCYCLE THREE:

CUSTOMER-FOCUSED ACCESS

Marketers who adapt to technology will have great advantage over those who don't.

Marketers who fail to embrace radical changes in how they reach their customers in the new century — and how individual customers access the information they want — will find themselves on the sidelines as a reborn marketing system steamrolls past.

That new marketing system focuses on the concept of how customers access information. It places pressure on marketers to provide numerous entrances or "portals" of access to information that are instantaneous, multi-channeled, totally integrated and presented at a level of sophistication that's required by the individual customer. It requires marketers to accept that the process of customer access is evolving from one described as "employee-assisted convenience" to one of "customer-determined application."

Due to technological advances, business and consumer customers already can use a number of methods to access marketing information and place orders — from traditional mail catalogs to telemarketing to direct, interactive computer links and everything in between. However, the addition of fiber optic technology in the new century, when combined with silicone intelligence, will cause a millionfold increase in the capacity for transmitting information and knowledge instantly and globally.

Multi-portal, customer-focused access is not only inevitable but logical. It's actually just an extension of other interactive technologies that are appearing due to customer demand, such as automated teller machines, direct-dial telephone systems, call direction systems, and interactive computer networks like CompuServe and Prodigy.

While multi-portal access now represents a small portion of some businesses' marketing techniques, marketers who recognize its potential will have a great advantage in technology and experience over those who don't.

THE PRINTED WORD GOES DIGITAL

Perhaps the most heretical prediction for the next century is that printed advertising will become obsolete within 25 years. To put this concept into perspective, however, consider that when companies were creating their business plans 25 years ago, there were no computers, software, or 800 and 900 telephone numbers, database management systems, telemarketing departments or desktop publishing capabilities. There also were no environmental concerns or privacy controversies. Federal Express hadn't yet altered the fundamental concept of time. In fact, many American businesses were not yet conceived, along with many modern jobs.

Technological progress demands a more immediate, efficient, inexpensive and environmentally-responsible means of transmitting information. We're on the edge of an interactive technological revolution that will encompass fiber optics, computers, telephones, television, cable, satellites, cellular communications, direct order access and a host of new customer access portals not yet conceived.

Yet here we are with an archaic advertising distribution system that relies on trucking pallets of product catalogs, flyers and magazines thousands of miles, sorting them into postal zones and carrier routes, and physically relaying our message to customers. We expend massive resources to establish alternative mail delivery systems to the U.S. Postal Service when the fiber optic transmission of electronic knowledge will make printed material inefficient and obsolete.

Also keep in mind that the American consumer has a unique capacity and ability to accept the fact that if something is possible they'll quickly adopt it to their business and personal worlds. If it's possible to have overnight delivery, it will become a standard. If it's possible to order on a credit card and get same-day shipment, it will become a standard. If it's possible to buy products interactively in business or at home, it will become the accepted standard. Americans love technology, convenience, instant gratification and speed.

SUBCYCLE: CONSORTIUM-BASED FULFILLMENT SYSTEMS

In order to effectively market products and services in this future of interactive technologies, companies will find it necessary to create consortiums — large groups of marketing companies that pool their resources to provide centralized access to large numbers of consumers in broadly defined niche markets. This consolidated system will provide an organized means for customers to access information and for companies to fulfill orders. Eventually this will eliminate the redundancies and expenses involved in individual corporate development.

■ ■ ■

Printed advertising will become obsolete within 25 years.

These consortiums will be linked together by a centralized, common database that would be interactive with millions of consumer or business-to-business buyers. Sound farfetched? Not only is it possible, it's already in existence in the forms of CompuServe and Prodigy in the United States, and in Minitel in France. Ultimately, such consortiums will be the model for the paradigmatic shift of the rebirth of marketing in the new century.

While the most obvious advantage of such consortiums to customers is the streamlined access to member companies with a higher standard of performance, the concept offers additional advantages to consortium members:

■ **Greater technological advances.** While consolidated and cooperative, consortiums would also preserve the individual corporation and thereby allow it to totally concentrate on product development, marketing, merchandising, knowledge-based customer focused and direct business stimulating activities.

With the expense of technological innovation spread across groups of companies, technological advances would evolve faster, better and with far greater efficiencies of time and investment costs.

■ **Combined resources.** It's conceivable that non-revenue producing activities such as accounting, inventory management and MIS services could be performed on a shared-service basis with one staff serving all the consortium members.

■ **Combined databases.** Consortium memberships, extended on a non-competing basis, would strengthen the management and use of creative database systems. If one database is good, 10 databases that are linked for continuity and knowledge are better. It's possible that memberships within large consortiums will be considered assets, similar to having a seat on the stock or commodity exchange.

■ **Greater profit opportunity.** Centralized management and human resources will eliminate costly redundancies, allowing individual corporate profits to rise. By providing a stable operating history, consortiums will become the focus of investment money; quite possibly selling shares in the consortium based on the profitability of its member companies.

■ **Greater buying power of services.** In time, individual member companies will look to consortiums for healthcare insurance, employee pension planning and administration, as well as legal and financial services. Major banks will form competitive alliances with consortiums, thereby offering a level of services to all members that could not be provided on an individual basis.

MICROCYCLE: DEVELOPING MULTI-PORTAL ACCESS FOR CUSTOMERS

Advanced direct marketers such as Penny Wise, the Maryland-based office products company, have already developed electronic catalogs on floppy disks which allow customers to place orders. The company advertises the speed and advantage of its on-line, direct order entry in its printed catalog, and then provides disks to customers with periodic product and price updates. Plus, Penny Wise also is found on the interactive CompuServe network.

All tolled, Penny Wise has four portals of access — mail, telephone, individual direct modem link and the CompuServe network link. With the exception of traditional mail order, Penny Wise offers customers the time-based advantage of instantaneous information and ordering.

■■■

Marketing is adding a new component: Electronic systems transmission.

Additional portals for marketers to consider are the potential offered by 900 numbers and cable TV systems. For example, through arrangements with AT&T and its credit services division, marketers could advertise and sell their products through a combination of 800 and 900 interactive systems.

The 800 number system provides the advertising component, then through a transfer option, the customer is switched to the 900 system to purchase the product. The marketer is paid immediately by AT&T and the customer is billed on the 900 number phone bill that provides options for selecting payment through direct pay or AT&T's universal credit card.

The cable TV system, interbred with the telephone and the computer, offers another portal option. In this case, the customer selects the business products channel and uses a menu to review a catalog of specific products. The customer then orders via an interactive, remote key pad using the order entry function and all shipping and billing information is already maintained on the cable system database. The business customer is invoiced by the cable service and receives one monthly, consolidated invoice rather than multiple invoices from multiple vendors.

Neither of these two portals of customer access are revolutionary or unusually innovative. In one way or another, they already exist. What's important to recognize, however, is that marketing is adding a new component (electronic systems transmission) and eliminating an old one (mail).

The new component that delivers the advertising and accepts the order is an interactive electronic system consisting of software, fiber optics and electronic interfaces. The old component being eliminated consists of an obsolete and expensive distribution infrastructure which is labor intensive, environmentally negative and that requires excessively complex and inefficient preparation procedures.

Perhaps most important, the use of interactive electronic systems eliminates the uncontrolled silent partner that has operated with impunity within each of our businesses for many years: the U.S. Postal Service.

The monopolistic franchise of the postal system limits the access to third-class mail. And that economic and physical constraint to trade freedom can't be tolerated in a technologically driven future in which customers place a premium on immediate and total access to information.

In order to remain a viable player in the interactive future ahead, your company must adapt to technology and make a commitment to developing multi-portal access systems for customers.

Anything less limits your customers' alternatives, and ensures that your company will become obsolete.

■ ■ ■

■ **Customer-Focused Access:** The third of ten supercycles for the new century. A supercycle is something that society has come to expect as a constant of commerce. Customer-focused access defines customers' expectations on the number of options available to access companies for information, and to place and have orders fulfilled.

■ **Consortium-Based Fulfillment Systems:** A subcycle of customer-focused access, which is defined as something specific that your industry can do to provide more efficient and effective access for customers. Consortiums are large groups of marketing companies that pool their resources to provide centralized access to large numbers of consumers in broadly defined niche markets.

■ **Multi-Portal Access Development:** A microcycle of customer-focused marketing. It's defined as a competitive strategy that your individual company can use to provide your customers with numerous entrances or "portals" of access to your company.

SUPERCYCLE FOUR:

CUSTOMER-FOCUSED FINANCE

The creative use of customer financing will open new frontiers for marketing innovation.

What's happened to long-term vision in American business? It's been traded in for a maniacal focus on short-term profitability. And as a result, it's forfeiting our country's ability to survive in a competitive global marketplace.

While American companies pay lip service to long-term investment, strategically oriented nations like Japan are putting tenacious teeth into it. Japan invests in long-term strategies that are planned 250 years into the future; and these plans describe short-term investment strategies that extend 30 to 40 years. How can U.S. corporations possibly expect to compete with their obsessive focus on next quarter's operating profits?

The decision facing our nation's business leaders is clear: Either begin to compete on a strategic par — through patient, overt and calculated long-term investment strategies — or risk losing markets piece by piece until they're completely gone.

Customer-focused finance could represent the awakening of reason and a return to the rational, long-term investment strategy that America desperately needs. Without it, American business can't rebuild the commercial infrastructure and lay the technological foundations for the future.

If companies continue to focus on the short-term, there may be increasing return on investment but ultimately, individual customers and markets will be lost. If companies truly focus on the long-term, they will realize little immediate return on investment, but they will retain customers. The choice is simple: Moderate the immediate profit expectation or lose the market. There is no strategic middle-ground.

The current corporate focus on short-term profitability has created a tremendous, energy-consuming financial structure. Not only has this produced an anemic research and development effort, but it has removed any focus on the creative use of finance for capturing market share and retaining customers. In short, too many accountants are making marketing decisions.

The new century will be a financial battleground in which wars will be fought more for regaining control of corporations from passive management, than for dominating the market. Once the strategic direction is returned to its proper perspective, customer-focused finance will be used as a marketing tool to capture market share and retain customers.

SUBCYCLE: CUSTOMER-FOCUSED FINANCIAL SERVICES

In the new century, finance will represent the genesis for bold and creative innovations in the development of market share. In this final frontier, invoicing will be obsolete, credit cards will be accepted for business-to-business purchasing, and you'll be working with payment systems that haven't yet been created. Individual purchases will be accredited into single, consolidated invoices for an entire month that offer the convenience and bookkeeping sanity of making only one payment.

In addition, the Price Club–type membership concept that has become a popular method of purchasing with consumers, will extend and evolve into the business purchasing arena as well. The sheer power of economy of scale makes this concept logical.

Controlling costs in a highly elastic environment is essential to maintaining a narrow edge of profitability. The combined purchasing power of thousands of businesses — joined through purchasing consortiums — is far greater than any individual company's negotiations could ever produce. Therefore, business-to-business marketers will increasingly sell into larger consolidations of cooperating buyers.

This type of "relational" marketing will emerge as the primary marketing strategy for the future. It involves establishing selling relationships with large organizational blocks such as memberships, associations and industry cooperatives. Central to this strategy will be customized, centralized pricing, invoicing and financing. Payment terms will become a product.

The Price Club model demonstrates that the key to relational marketing is cost advantage. For example, Price Club members can save up to 50 percent of the retail cost of grocery and household items, which is an irresistible advantage to the consumer. The Price Club is much more interested in selling millions of $25 annual memberships than it is in margins.

Beyond the simple price advantage provided by Price Club–type operations, exists the frontier of creative financial service adjuncts.

Today, many corporations have turned over their payroll function to companies like ADP because it's more efficient and cost-effective. Using the ADP model, the entire accounts payable as accounts receivable functions could also be better administered at less cost by using external financial service organizations. While a large business-to-business marketing company might require 15 people to operate such departments, most of the work is routine, scheduled and standard. It lends itself to a system that is driven by database and efficient technology.

FRONTIER THINKING ENSURES FUTURE SURVIVAL

An excellent model of this concept is found in Integrated Credit Management Services, a Washington, DC–based financial services company. Its founders recognized three futurist concepts:

1. Customer retention is a critical issue;

2. Accounts receivable staffing will become too expensive; and

3. Financing of postage costs is an increasing need among its clients, who are direct marketers.

In developing a unique, advanced strategy for its clients, ICMS focused on customer retention as the key to collecting overdue accounts. The company substituted the old model for collection with a softer, "let's find a way that works for everybody" program that is focused on recovering the customer and the money. Customers are made to feel that the direct marketing company truly has an interest in working out the overdue bills in a way that assures they can continue to do business.

In addition to this program approach, ICMS can set up a total accounts receivable service for its clients that begins with the first invoice and follows through to the ultimate collection of delinquent accounts. And ICMS' banking affiliations allow them to manage accounts receivable for their direct marketing clients.

As a by-product, this provides advance postage financing which is then paid back from the client's receivables. This allows the company's clients to finance the high, up-front postage costs and to pay down the short-term loan through receivables.

This creative use of financial services represents the type of frontier thinking that allows companies to remain focused on their primary business and to ensure their future survival.

MICROCYCLE: CUSTOMER-FOCUSED, TERMS-BASED PRICING

Individual companies will explore and experiment with multiple-tier pricing in the next decade in an effort to focus on the strategic advantage of financing for their customers. Marketers will tailor pricing based on a menu of payment terms, partially in response to the threat of widespread, massive discounting in the immediate future.

For example, prices displayed in a catalog might list anywhere from two to five different prices for the same product, along with the variable quantity pricing at each tier. Immediate same-day funds transfer payment will receive the lowest pricing of the multi-tier systems, while 10 day terms on up to 30-, 60- and 90-day terms will command progressively higher prices. In essence, companies will finance their customers for a price; and they will use payment terms as a merchandising technique.

The net effect will be an increase in order frequency, a decrease in accounts receivable aging and a decrease in margin. The margin, however, is partially made up by the higher prices that are charged for longer payment terms.

Marketers could use price attraction as a prospecting technique at any of the multiple levels of price to uncover several possibilities.

For instance, a customer might be offered a 60-day pay period, while receiving the price afforded a 10-day payment term.

Marketers can then track and analyze individual customer responses to choices and payment terms, and their payment performance, to generate analyses of credit trends and to isolate credit risks from the database.

Multi-tier pricing and customized terms point directly to the imminent need for tailoring financial alternatives for each individual customer. The creative use of price and financing will open new territories for marketing innovation and attracting new customers.

■■■

SUPERCYCLE SUMMARY

■ **Customer-Focused Finance:** The fourth of ten supercycles for the new century. It will be used as a long-term investment and marketing tool to capture market share and retain customers.

■ **Customer-Focused Financial Services:** A subcycle of customer-focused finance which is defined as something specific your industry can do to provide financial services for your customers. This could include Price Club–type memberships with centralized pricing, invoicing and financing.

■ **Customer-Focused, Terms-Based Financing:** A microcycle of customer-focused finance. It is defined as a competitive strategy that your individual company can apply as a response to customer-focused finance. This could include multiple-tier pricing and payment systems.

SUPERCYCLE FIVE:

CUSTOMER-FOCUSED BUNDLING

Hypermarket memberships will be a boon to reaching customers.

In the new century, efficient marketing companies will have the best of all worlds: independence, enhanced operating efficiencies, time and space for product development, and the ability to concentrate on their individual customer at the individual customer level. Sound like a dream come true? Actually, this scenario is a very real and attainable by-product that comes as a result of a new focus that will change the shape of marketing for all time:

Hypermarketing.

Undoubtedly, you've heard the term before. The rise of the office supply superstore is an example of one small, tentative step toward the future of "bundling" goods and services for customers. But what we'll see in the new century will go far beyond this budding hypermarket concept.

Marketers in the new century will provide their customers with ever-increasing menus of goods and services under one umbrella — a kind of cooperative vendor relationship that is comprised of hundreds of participating suppliers. These memberships will form along affinity lines by industry, such as the electrical manufacturing, construction and health care industries. Ultimately, competition among memberships will be determined by their degree and quality of instantaneity, their knowledge, access and financial services available to their members.

The make up of these memberships will be based on what individual companies can bring to the party, how their participation will provide the end customer with the greatest breadth and depth of products and services. Companies will be invited to become members based on the attraction of their unique product or niche.

These coveted positions will extend into multiple memberships, allowing marketers to own positions that will extend their market share in the way that acquisitions do today. Several things will occur as this supercycle of hypermarketing develops:

1. Marketers will gradually relinquish the fulfillment-related portions of their business to the memberships, which can best accomplish this on a shared-service basis. For example, warehousing and fulfillment will be done on a consolidated basis for large numbers of individual companies. By sharing staff, facilities, material handling, hardware and software systems companies will reduce these labor-intensive elements.

2. The burden of new customer development and acquisition will shift to the membership. This will allow individual companies the financial time and space to concentrate on product development, customer relations, advertising and technological advancement.

3. Routinely purchased goods and services will be negotiated by the membership for the common benefit of its non-competing

members, providing pricing advantages that couldn't be achieved individually. The membership will handle contracts for shipping, pre-press services, printing, paper buying, media advertising, telephone services, health care and other products and services.

Bottom line, the economies of scale across every operating component of business provide member companies with an enormous advantage: A conglomerate operating economy with individualized ownership. Their end customers benefit, too, from numerous other efficiencies — controlled, competitive pricing, single source access for a variety of goods and services, centralized invoicing, combined shipping and freight savings.

In the final analysis, hypermarketing structures made up of stable, profitable, independent companies are better for the global economy than highly consolidated, centrally-owned conglomerates.

SUBCYCLE: COOPERATIVE ADVERTISING

The first step toward creating a hypermarketing structure is to identify several non-competing marketing companies that can work cooperatively and on a shared-advertising basis offer their collective customers additional goods and services. Key to the proper utilization of shared advertising is, of course, a willingness to open up and share databases. Plus, a readjustment of attitudes toward the supposed sacrosanctity of an individual company's advertising.

■ ■ ■

Marketing is long past the old school philosophy of total isolation and secrecy.

As an industry, marketing is long past the old school philosophy of total isolation and secrecy. If common database administration and analyses are to be accepted in the ultimate development of a hypermarket, then sharing customer database information on a one-to-one, cooperative advertising basis is where it must begin. This is the critical pathway, etched through trust and integrity, that brings cooperative efforts to fruition.

Cooperative advertising begins by exchanging offers in each others' advertising so that numerous databases can be reached. From there, the possibilities are not only infinite, but exciting. For example:

■ Each company can recommend or endorse the other companies to their customers, explaining why the recommendation was made and what the other companies can do for the customer.

■ All the cooperating companies might agree on advantageous payment terms or automatically extend account services to customers.

■ All cooperating companies might agree to offer each new customer an incentive such as "buy from one company and get an introductory 25 percent discount" from the other member companies.

Nothing marks an old school marketer more quickly than the attitudes about advertising space. It's treated as commercial real estate or some form of personal and sacred temple. In the new century, the exposure to the qualified databases from numerous other marketers will be worth far more than the paltry net profit (if any) from their least productive advertising. Don't waste time trying to convince arthritic companies of the advantages of cooperative advertising. Instead, seek out innovators with the energy and vision to firmly place themselves among the practitioners of the new science and art of marketing.

MICROCYCLE: CO-MAILING & CO-PROCESSING

While co-mailing has been done by advanced direct marketers and printers such as Quad/Graphics for the past six years, only a small number of companies have been able to join cooperatively to take advantage of the savings. Usually there's resistance to the change, an inability to agree on trim sizes and inflexibility about mail dates.

However, with postage increases a constant reality for marketers, it will be necessary to form mailing consortiums that include large numbers of mailers who are intent on getting the maximum possible savings. Co-mailing, by itself, doesn't represent a significant microcycle within the industry. It does, however, stand as an indication of the important influence at work: Cooperation. And as a result of cooperation, consortium members will find additional logical extensions. Those who now participate in co-mailing will join together to handle other routine and repetitive functions — from shared mail processing and paper buying to pre-press and print production services.

■ ■ ■

SUPERCYCLE SUMMARY

■ **Customer-Focused Bundling:** The fifth of ten supercycles for the new century. Customer-focused bundling describes the development of hypermarket "memberships" in which hundreds of marketers will provide their customers with a vast menu of products and services under one umbrella. By-products of this cooperation include better operating efficiencies, savings in membership purchases like mailing, paper buying, etc., and more time and dollars for product development.

■ **Cooperative Advertising:** A subcycle of customer-focused bundling which is defined as something specific your industry can do to reach customers. In this case, several non-competing companies can cooperate on a share advertising basis to offer their collective customers additional goods and services. Key to doing so is the sharing of databases and a change in attitude about advertising space.

■ **Co-Mailing & Co-Processing:** A micro-cycle of customer-focused bundling, which is defined as a competitive strategy that your individual company can apply. For example, your company can cooperate with non-competing companies to purchase products and services at group "membership" rates (such as co-mailing and co-processing, pre-press and print production services).

SUPERCYCLE SIX:

CUSTOMER-FOCUSED SERVICES DELIVERY

The marketing commandment of the new century will be "Thou Shalt Not Schlep."

Marketers need a new vision of what it means to deliver products and services to customers. One that goes beyond the obvious, beyond the inadequate, beyond the usual and customary. You must zero in on the psyche of the customer and figure out how to do more things that the customer can no longer continue to do well. You need to find entire new frontiers of service delivery that will turn entire industries upside down and inside out.

Increasingly, time-starved customers will gravitate to full-service trade and delivery systems that don't require them to go out, to drive, to load, to carry, or to set up and maintain the products and services they've purchased. You company's ability to develop delivery systems without restrictions of size, weight, time or distance will become synonymous with performance and convenience in your customers' eyes. Your vision of such delivery systems will forever alter the commercial act of trade and service.

On-site services for customers will become an important factor in differentiating your company, particularly as technology proliferates and processes become more sophisticated. Both will outrace the individual customer's ability and capacity to assimilate.

Consider, for example, the time spent inside your business by service providers from the computer, copier, shipping and telecommunications industries, and you begin to realize that this trend exists. Then project it into an almost exclusively interactive, electronic, database-dominated environment and you being to realize the trend's magnitude.

A STROKE OF GENIUS

A superb example of this supercycle is embodied in the concept of CallTrack, a telecommunications services company that targets businesses that want to control their telephone usage costs. Traditionally, companies have had to shuffle through hundreds of pages of telephone call records from the monthly phone bill and still know nothing about what was going on inside the company. CallTrack recognized that time-starved managers had no interest in either schlepping through the phone bill or hiring staff to do tedious analysis.

In a stroke of entrepreneurial genius, CallTrack developed a highly sophisticated, advanced software system that examines and measures every outgoing call by each department and each employee. The system then produces a series of concise, understandable executive reports each month that pinpoint waste, inefficiency and abuse. In short, for as little as a $10 a month service fee, an executive can review the company's entire phone activity in about 15 minutes — and know everything about who is using the telephone system and have the information to do something about it.

CallTrack services go beyond, too. They set up every employee with the opportunity to automatically charge their personal calls to their personal credit card. Thus, the company is spared having to confront the employee and having to collect money for personal telephone calls made at the business.

The companies using CallTrack experience savings at multiple levels. For example, a company with an average $1,000 monthly long distance phone bill that is paying 24 cents per minute and has 20 employees making long distance calls found that their average business call lasted about 3½ minutes, while their average personal call lasted six minutes.

After putting CallTrack to work, the company reported 10 percent fewer business calls and 10 percent shorter business calls. The personal calls dropped by 50 percent, they were 33 percent shorter and, most important, the personal calls were paid for by the employees. The overall savings amounted to 257 hours of productivity time or about $3,850, plus another $3,800 on the business and personal call charges. The total savings: $7,650. The cost: About $500 for CallTrack.

CallTrack also sells top quality AT&T long distance telephone service and matches the rates charged by other carriers. The company sells long distance time to many customers as a primary business, but their marketing strategy is total services delivery and reporting systems.

True to the supercycle, CallTrack doesn't require the customer to do anything. Once the decision is made to sign up, it just happens. That is pure customer-focused services delivery and the type of vision that is necessary to embrace this super-cycle.

SUBCYCLE: IMPLOSION EXPANSION OF SERVICES

Marketers in the new century need to see themselves through a futurist's telescope and recognize the power of a "black hole." At the center of a black hole, matter and gravity reach immense density. The power is awesome, foreboding and indestructible. That is the analogous potential for the marketing industry in the new century and the new millennium.

The subcycle of "implosion expansion of services" demands that marketing literally implodes into itself in order to create maximum density.

The airline industry, for example, missed an opportunity to implode its service delivery by not operating their own airport limousine shuttle services, valet parking services, long-term airport parking services and flight insurance services. Inside their terminals, they missed an implosion opportunity by not creating their own restaurants where high-quality food and service would capture the public's interest.

The airlines didn't go deep within the customer and accompany that person on every last detail of a business or personal trip. Implode into the travel customer and you'll find no less than 100 new service delivery opportunities waiting to be activated and profited from.

This subcycle offers every advanced marketer an opportunity to create *retrospectively*, which is an important distinction. We have very little information that can be acted upon regarding where a customer is going. But by taking a retrospective view — through the experience of the individual customer — it is possible to determine where that customer has been just prior to reaching our companies.

That's where the implosion of service delivery can take place. Work your way back through the customer's commercial pathway and you'll find incredible instances where no one met or even recognized that customer's many needs.

The secret to imploding as a new marketing paradigm is to listen, to hear what is being said, and then to have the fortitude to take bold steps and do something about what your customer has just told you.

MICROCYCLE: CUSTOMER OPPORTUNITY MAPPING

The old school of marketing became impatient and disenchanted with classic market research techniques in the late 1980s. As a result, marketers fell back on the safety of numbers and conservative accounting-based conclusions when it came to customer and market opportunities. Consequently, the equivalent of the nuclear winter descended when the fallout from increased postage and UPS rates swept over the industry in early 1991 at the height of the nation's recession.

Market research, as a deservedly maligned discipline, will come into favor once again only by "getting a life." Marketers going into the frenetic new century aren't interested in the dry bones of hypothetical models that represent abstract caricatures of customers. They want the blood, flesh and the living and beating heart of the individual customer who is ready to buy *now*.

■■■

*Go out and meet
the biggest asset you have:
your customers.*

As a microcycle of implosion and customer-focused service delivery, "customer opportunity mapping" will first be done by individual companies. Then, ultimately, by born-again market research companies that will seek out real customers who buy real products from real companies.

To get a jump on marketing's re-enactment of Lewis and Clark, put good people on the road right now to go out and meet the biggest asset you have: your customers. Forget research models with perfectly constructed questions. Forget what the people in the executive suite are saying; they haven't got a clue as to what's going on with customers. Sit down with 1,000 different customers in 1,000 different towns across the country, have a cup of coffee and find out what is really happening with your business, products and services.

As a marketing executive, what percentage of your time should be spent in direct, face-to-face customer dialogue? If you believe that even a paltry 15 percent of your work year is enough, that means you should be spending a full 37 days a year talking to real customers. Do you?

Sooner or later you are going to have to do hands-on, straight-from-the-hip, down-and-dirty customer opportunity mapping. During the past few years CEOs have quietly been putting on plaid shirts and leaving on extended sabbaticals to roam the customer circuit. These rare individuals know what is coming and they're going to be prepared. They have a long-term vision for their companies and consider customer opportunity more important than meetings fretting about next quarter's short-term profits.

There are only five important landmarks on any customer opportunity mapping expedition. They will never let you down and will get you where you hope to go. More than ever before, the new century demands that we respect them:

1. In the beginning, there must be margins.

2. You are in the business of creating and keeping customers.

3. Quality is free; service is profit.

4. Look for holes.

5. Be obsessed with individual customers.

■ ■ ■

SUPERCYCLE SUMMARY

■ **Customer-Focused Services Delivery:** The sixth of ten supercycles for the new century. In the future, the delivery of services will assume an entire new dynamic. It will become synonymous with convenience and performance, and will be an assumed component of the products and services your customers purchase.

■ **Implosion Expansion Of Services:** A subcycle of customer-focused services delivery which is defined as something specific your industry can do to provide services to your customers. This involves taking a retrospective view — through the experience of the individual customer — to determine where the customer has been prior to reaching your company. Working you way through this commercial pathway reveals instances where no one met or recognized the customer's many and varied needs.

■ **Customer Opportunity Mapping:** A microcycle of customer-focused services delivery which is defined as a competitive strategy that your individual company can apply as a response to customer-focused services delivery. This might include research of individual customers by market research companies that focus on real buyers (rather than hypothetical models) and doing your own face-to-face dialogue with customers to find out what is happening with your business, products and services.

SUPERCYCLE SEVEN:

CUSTOMER-FOCUSED ADVERTISING

Electronic advertising, solicited by consumers, is the wave of things to come.

Your ability to remain at the forefront of the consumer's awareness — *without the use of physical, printed advertising or telephone contact* — will mark your success as a marketer in the new century. Meeting that immense challenge will be equivalent to battling a nuclear war with a BB gun for those who aren't prepared to take on their new role in the marketing arena.

For years marketers have relied on the use of mass, unsolicited printed mailings to advertise goods and services to their customers. But that approach is coming to an end in the new century and it's clear what's next: A restructuring of the whole future of direct marketing.

High costs of mass mailings and poor response rates from saturated consumers are just two of the factors supporting the need for change. This supercycle is being driven into being on a "lesser of two evils" level by a host of factors — the access to interactive, electronic marketing tools, consumer's growing concerns over privacy and advertising "noise", environmental issues and legislative momentum.

Privacy and environmental responsibility are both "apple pie" legislative issues and are therefore perceived as "good" by the public and elected politicians. Marketers using direct marketing techniques are perceived to be the evil perpetrators of the "flood of unwanted, privacy-invading, environment-damaging junk mail."

There's more to this than first meets the eye. First, privacy is a Constitutional issue and one that would be difficult to legislate. The environment, on the other hand, is an emotional issue and one that is more easily legislated. If the intent is to control privacy rights, then the easiest way to do so is through environmental legislation.

Consider this scenario. Businesses and consumers are presented with two options: Either elect to continue receiving "junk mail" and pay a substantial landfill tax for its disposal, or elect not to receive "junk mail." If significant economic sanctions are legislated, which choice do you believe the average business and average consumer will make?

■■■

Marketers are perceived to be the evil perpetrators of junk mail.

The answer is less important than the process. The process will, by default, eliminate so many names from the universe that rentals will skyrocket and direct marketers will face an untenable economic reality. Keep in mind that the Mail Preference Service — the "take me off the all mailing lists" list — has experienced a 43 percent jump in requests since Earth Day 1990. And it's still increasing at an alarming rate.

The potential is serious. And its exacerbated by the industry's perception. Consider the overall image of "mail order" and "direct marketing" and "telemarketing." How well have we addressed ourselves and our industry to the 98 percent of recipients who still throw us away? How well has the industry done in organizing national efforts to fend off these negative perceptions and lack of respect? Look at the number of legislative proposals and bills before the Federal and state legislatures and the provincial legislatures of Canada that are specifically designed to limit direct marketing in one way or another. There is a groundswell of serious magnitude and very little is being done.

To survive well into the next century, the structure of direct marketing must involve reversing advertising from unsolicited to solicited, from marketer-driven to consumer-driven. It will require that advertising become electronic, which is non-polluting, environmentally neutral and easily controlled by the individual.

SUBCYCLE: EXPORTING THE OLD DIRECT MARKETING CONCEPTS

Whenever the U.S. bans a pesticide or chemical, we generally don't stop selling it; instead, we export it to countries having no prohibitions. We're now seeing the first wholesale exportation of North American direct marketing and it will continue to grow into the new century. It's all over the European landscape. It will grow dramatically in the emerging first world nations of South America. It's already spread to Japan and will be adapted to all of Asia (and North Americans won't be running the show).

Bottom line, direct marketing follows response. Rather than decreasing on a global basis, direct marketing is only in its infancy. U.S. direct marketing is maturing relative to response, satu-ration and the country's competitive homogene-ity. U.S. direct marketers, however, will go where the growth is — engaging in a prolonged and serious exportation of the most advanced marketing industry in the world.

This exportation will require marketers to main-tain two technologies of advertising. In the U.S.

and Canada, advertising will be interactive, fiber-optic and solicited. Elsewhere, advertising will be reruns of the 1980s and 1990s, at least for a period of years. The profits from the overt colonization by North American marketers will be used to leverage the industry to a new plateau of sophistication and technological wonder. Then the whole cycle will repeat itself, as we export electronic, interactive direct marketing to emerging first world countries.

MICROCYCLE: EXPERIMENTING IN THE INTERNATIONAL SCENE

The current trend among established and well-funded business-to-business and consumer marketers is to experiment with international operations. Those experiments vary from start ups and joint ventures to partnerships or acquisitions. It's too early to determine which of these international expansion models will dominate, but each has positive aspects and significant drawbacks.

The commitment to Europe has been, for some, expensive and not terribly rewarding; for others, it's passed muster. The number of international direct marketers is, in reality, still limited (outside of the Fortune 500 and 1000 Club) but is growing each year. The "magic of 1992" which propelled early exportation has somewhat cooled to become a "maybe of 1995 or 1999." There are numerous barriers to overcome, particularly in the areas of international delivery systems, corporate organizational structures and the vast number of diverse target markets.

The years immediately ahead of us, when taken in the broad cycle of global business expansion, must be viewed as the early experimentation years. Thus far, it's clear that it becomes increasingly difficult to look to international expansion as the only logical source of growth.

If there is one thing that the smart marketing visionaries have learned, it's this: The market is global and nobody owns the customer.

■ ■ ■

■ **Customer-Focused Advertising**: The seventh of ten supercycles for the new century. Customer-focused advertising describes a complete restructuring of direct marketing that makes advertising solicited rather than unsolicited, consumer-driven rather than company-driven, electronic and interactive rather than produced with paper and ink.

■ **Exportation of Marketing Concepts**: A subcycle of customer-focused advertising which is defined as something specific your industry can do to reach customers. While U.S. direct marketing is maturing relative to response, American marketers will begin exporting their expertise to European countries, Japan, and a host of third world nations. The profits from this exportation effort will be used to leverage industry growth to a new level of sophistication and technological advancement in the U.S.

■ **Experimenting Internationally**: A microcycle of customer-focused advertising, which is defined as a competitive strategy that your individual company can apply. Start ups, joint ventures, partnerships or acquisitions offer your company a variety of ways to test the international waters, but it's too early yet to determine which will be most rewarding.

SUPERCYCLE EIGHT:

CUSTOMER-FOCUSED DATABASES

Pooled database information will herald the future of true integrated, database marketing.

In the future you'll use an artificial database that your customers participate in creating and you'll share it with numerous other companies. With this tool you will determine the projected line item budget and the probable purchases of an individual consumer or business customer one year in advance. And your projections will have a reliability factor of plus or minus one percent. Is this reality or "beam-me-up-Scotty" time?

The ability of multiple companies to pool database information to reach mutually beneficial, non-competitive marketing objectives will herald the future of true integrated, database marketing. Knowing the customer will take on new degrees of meaning, because consumers themselves will select to what level and to what degree they will participate in the information-gathering process. And, with artificial intelligence, shared customer knowledge will totally redefine the present two-dimensional concept of segmentation.

The development of such extensive databases will emerge as a by-product of consumers' membership in hyper-marketing "pods", groups composed of suppliers of goods and services. As advertising reverses from unsolicited to solicited, consumers will become more aware of the need to provide personal information that will improve the level of services and the appropri-ateness of the goods they are offered. As a result, their participation in the creation of a database will become voluntary and non-invasive.

The individual consumer or business customer will determine the degree of their participation, as well as how the personal information will be used and expanded.

Consumers, for example, might allow marketers to develop a complete database dossier on their sports interests, purchases and preferences, but will limit the construction of a dossier on their video viewing interests. No longer will companies rent names. Instead, they will rent databases that range from unsophisticated names and information to moderately enhanced databases with purchasing histories to fully-loaded databases with analyzed dossiers and predictive models of purchasing preferences.

■ ■ ■

No longer will companies rent names; they will rent databases.

The ideal customer of the new century will have the total purchasing and product preference history of the past 10 years encoded on a magnetic strip. This customer, for a fee, will allow selected marketing pods to access that information and to use it to develop modeled purchasing protocols — one-year purchasing plans that will centralize all buying into one "program" of total marketing service for that individual customer.

Participatory database management will operate in the rare atmosphere of several dimensions — 15 companies studying the same members from 15 different perspectives — that will open opportunities rather than limit them.

SUBCYCLE: DATABASE ASSEMBLY

Today an individual customer may exist in the databases of 50 different companies. With database assembly techniques, these companies will be able to pool their information to create a conglomerate history of consumers and business customers that will establish such things as:

- purchasing preferences;

- price level information and preferences;

- overall returns;

- intercompany loyalty patterns;

- seasonality activity and "power purchase" periods;

- financial stability projections;

- chains of associated buyers within the company or family.

This will allow marketers to see customers through 50 different records and to create multi-dimensional "Purchase Resonance Imaging," much like the views of the human body that are made by CAT Scan and Magnetic Resonance Imaging. The nuances and subtleties of each customer's behavior that will be gained by marketers will elevate the concept of customer focusing to near-predictive surety.

MICROCYCLE: INVEST NOW IN ARTIFICIAL INTELLIGENCE

The database that *learns* has already captured the interest of a few advanced marketers. But at the individual company level, it's becoming clear that once this technological state of grace is reached, it will probably be obsolete. The speed of technology is simply too fast for marketers to respond to.

That's why it makes sense to invest heavily and go straight into an artificial intelligence database now — rather than obtaining a relational database in the next couple of years that will soon be outdated. It's better to eliminate the intervening pain of once again arriving at the party only to find out that it was last week.

■ ■ ■

SUPERCYCLE SUMMARY

■ **Customer-Focused Participatory Databases:** The eighth of ten supercycles for the new century. In the future, your customers will participate in the development of your databases, determine the degree of their participation, and how the personal information will be used and expanded.

■ **Database Assembly:** A subcycle of customer-focused participatory databases which is defined as something specific your industry can do to provide products and services to your customers. This involves pooling customer information with several other companies to create a conglomerate history of customers.

■ **Investing In Artificial Intelligence:** A microcycle of customer-focused participatory databases which is defined as a competitive strategy that your individual company can apply as a response to this supercycle. Rather than investing in technology that will soon be outdated, it's better to invest now in a database that learns.

SUPERCYCLE NINE:

CUSTOMER-FOCUSED COMMON MARKETS

North, Central and South America will be the marketplace of the new century.

Marketers in the new century will be challenged to alter the way they think about market expansion, as the North American Common Market emerges and ultimately evolves into the North-South American Common market. Specifically, marketers will need to focus on:

■ moving from horizontal expansion to vertical expansion;

■ from U.S. marketing dominance to Pan-Americas marketing dominance;

- from integrated socio-economic marketing to discrete and separate socio-economic marketing;

- from English speaking to Spanish speaking;

- from conventional strategy to unconventional strategy;

- from a conservative to a risk-taking approach in financing.

- from a sure return on investment to a future return on investment.

In the new century, marketers with the capacity, resources and time for ROI financing will operate on a Pan American basis — from North and Central to South America, the marketplace of the new century.

To dominate this market will require large investments of capital, people, time and patience. The reborn concept of customer-focused marketing will have multiple definitions and economic levels that are different from those of its purely North American history. Consolidation will reach new heights within marketing; the economies of a Pan-American operating scale will dictate the speed and aggressiveness of multi-national expansion.

The first area of expansion will be Mexico. The free trade agreement carries with it many considerations — geo-political, demographic, immigration and socio-economic — that are far and away more compelling than the pure trade benefits that are initially apparent. Mexico and the U.S. are joined at the hip in an inescapable tide of cultural change; there can be no turning back for Mexico if it is to finally emerge as a first world nation. For the U.S., the intraculturization is the trade-off for a strong North-South American Common Market and, in the final analysis, freedom from Asian market dominance.

■ ■ ■

Great immigration movements will occur in the next two decades.

The second area of expansion will be South America. While Mexico looks to the United

States, South America will look to Mexico. Of all the third world countries, the South American economies are the most developed and poised for almost immediate transformation to first world economies. Plus the sheer size of the market is compelling.

Third will come Central America. Political instability will give way to the Mexican and South American vice grip and, grudgingly, Central America will join the Americas Common Market or it will be left out of the economic expansion it can't afford.

Great immigration movements will occur in the next two decades and there will be tremendous shifts in ethnic populations. The transition won't be easy, but it almost has to happen if the U.S. is to maintain a hold on global trade. The U.S. population is aging while the Mexican and South American populations are growing younger. Politically, the U.S. must have markets and politically, the Mexican, Central and South American countries must have employment for their youth or face devastating social unrest and rebellion.

SUBCYCLE: AGGRESSIVE SPANISH MARKET DEVELOPMENT

U.S. marketers who are wise to invest in developing markets will seek out the Spanish-speaking markets in the U.S. first, and then turn their expansion attention to Mexico. To some degree, the U.S. Spanish markets will be used as the experimental lab for future initiatives in Mexico and South America.

MICROCYCLE: BILINGUAL STAFFING

Within a short amount of time, the Spanish language will be common within marketing departments and in entire industries. It's projected that Spanish will be equally dominant with English by the year 2020.

Within five years, it will be routine that staffing will include Spanish-speaking employees. Already, numerous companies are staffing their order and customer service departments with bilingual, native Spanish-speaking employees. Marketing professionals are also beginning to realize that their own ability to speak Spanish will be an important qualification in advancing their careers.

■ ■ ■

SUPERCYCLE SUMMARY

■ **Customer-Focused Common Markets:** The ninth of ten supercycles. The North American common market will evolve into the North-South American common market.

■ **Aggressive Spanish Market Development:** A subcycle of customer-focused common markets. U.S. companies will first invest in developing Spanish-speaking markets in the U.S. and then will use their knowledge to expand into Mexico and South America.

■ **Bilingual Staffing:** A microcycle of aggressive Spanish market development. To serve the Pan American market, all employees (including marketing professionals) will need to be bilingual.

SUPERCYCLE TEN:

CUSTOMER-FOCUSED, SELF-GENERATED SUPERCYCLES

Customers will recapture and regain control of the process of trade.

The most striking reversal of marketing in the future is that customers will recognize that control is theirs for the taking. Once the process of trade is placed in the participating hands of customers, they will take control and define each successive step of the future. Marketers will simply move in harmony with them. In essence, the rebirth of marketing into customer-focused marketing will reach a state of Taoist philosophy — the seller will flow with the buyer, the buyer will flow with the seller and both will revolve in harmony.

This supercycle is filled with the greatest hope and the greatest danger for marketing. At issue here is control. All of the supercycles we've discussed have, in one way or another, illustrated increasing customer control. Whether this final supercycle emerges as influential depends on what response we as marketers make to the customer.

■ ■ ■

Customers will recognize
that control is theirs
for the taking.

From this point until the new century begins, the most disturbing issues we will face are being generated by our customers, not the marketing industry. A great deal of responsibility is implied in our response to those issues. We have the ability to determine the future of our industry, a future that can easily go one of two directions. Let's hope that it remains dedicated, first, to the benefit, satisfaction and service of our customers

■ ■ ■

CONCLUSION

Ahead of us lies a rebirth.

We have witnessed the emergence of marketing from its infancy and are now struggling with the problems of its childhood, complete with illnesses and frustrations.

Marketing is transforming, developing from a blank face of innocent infancy to the serious, experienced face of youth. It carries with it the heritage of the past, but its vision is set on the future. It has the innate capacity and capability to create solutions to every obstacle it encounters and to gain strength from overcoming adversity.

Marketing's ultimate adulthood lies out there, in the new century. And as we approach it, it will move even further into the reality of yet another future.

But when we arrive at the next level of maturity in time, we will have guided this industry through the most incredible advances ever experienced in its comparatively short life. We will be the next generation of parents to watch our child grow, mature and move faster into the future than we are able to. We will hand it on and it will become even larger, even fuller, even stronger. We will have succeeded.

■■■

ABOUT THE AUTHOR

Donald R. Libey is president of The Libey Consultancy, Inc., a marketing and strategic planning consultancy and seminar production firm. He also is publisher, president and CEO of Libey Publishing Incorporated, a trade publisher of business and marketing books, audio and video programs; president of Regnery Gateway, Inc., one of the most influential U.S. publishers of public policy, current events and political books; and founder and chairman of the North American Society For Strategic Marketing, marketing's first futurist think tank and publishing society concerned with the advanced, strategic futurist issues facing the industry.

Mr. Libey publishes a series of newsletters such as *The Libey New Century Letters* and *The Libey Letter* with more than a thousand readers. With a background in domestic and international direct marketing that includes consumer, healthcare, financial, investment, non-profit, business-to-business and publishing, he has been associated with major international marketing corporations and Fortune 500 companies in positions from marketing to the board of directors.

One of marketing's most outspoken, provocative and high-energy speakers and authors, Mr. Libey presents more than 70 hard-hitting seminars and keynote speeches at premier industry conferences in the U.S., Canada and Mexico each year. His speaking schedule includes keynote and featured speeches for the National Center For Database Marketing Annual Conference, the Annual Direct Marketing To Business National Conference, both the U.S. and the Canadian Direct Marketing Association Conferences, *Potentials In Marketing* Magazine's annual High Performance Marketing Conference, *Target Marketing's* Marketing To Europe and Canada Conference, and numerous other industry associations.

Mr. Libey's futurist concepts and articles appear frequently in the major North American trade publications. He writes for *Operations and Fulfillment* Magazine and is a contributing editor to *Potentials in Marketing* Magazine.

Available from Lakewood Books

LIBEY ON CUSTOMERS

Libey On Customers presents a futurist's view of the way customers will be created and retained through customer-focused marketing. Focusing totally on the customer creates levels of confidence, satisfaction, and loyalty that assure survival in the increasingly hostile and cut-throat business environment that will emerge across North America by the turn of the century. For CEOs and CEOs-to-be of direct marketing companies, retail companies, service organizations, and any business that needs customers for success, *Libey On Customers* provides the provocative foundation of customer-focused survival philosophy and thought for the new century.

Hardbound, 304 pages, $65.00

LIBEY ON SUPERFORCES

Libey On Superforces is a futurist's disturbing look at the massive social, political, cultural and economic forces that will tear apart and redefine North American business-to-business and consumer marketing in the crisis-dominated new century. Libey applies political and social forces to the trends supercycles and trends in marketing. He describes a collision of social and business superforces that will alter forever the way business is done. This is a book for every CEO and executive who is concerned about the fabric of business and commerce and what can be done to prepare new, alternative strategies.

Hardbound, 300 pages, $65.00
(Available December 1993)

LIBEY ON RECENCY, FREQUENCY AND MONETARY VALUE

Libey on Recency, Frequency and Monetary Value is an in-depth study of the patterns and performance of customer buying. Traditional analyses of when, how often, and how much a customer buys are no longer adequate. Using formulaic approaches, Libey describes analytic approaches to optimize and segment customer databases and to wring every bit of potential lifetime value and lifetime profit possible out of customer performance. This is a milestone book that clearly explains how to use recency, frequency and monetary value to improve profitability significantly. Less than 10% of North American marketing organizations use or even know about the concepts in this book.

Hardbound, 198 pages, $50.00
(Available December 1993)

MILLION DOLLAR MAILING$
by Denison Hatch

Million dollar mailings are just that: long-running consumer and direct mail packages that have proven themselves successful by bringing in millions of dollars in sales. The 71 all-time best mailings ever produced are fully illustrated and analyzed by their original creators. The result is an exclusive insider's look at the art and science of direct mail creative techniques, copy approaches, design, formats, offers — unlike anything ever before assembled. Hatch reveals the single most successful mailings in the history of the world — a package that has produced over *$1 billion* in sales. This book contains a million dollars worth of marketing information, know-how and wisdom.

Hardbound, 480 pages, illustrated, $89.00

U.S. DIRECT MARKETING LAW
by Richard Leighton and Alfred Regnery

Expert attorneys in the field of advertising and direct marketing law, Leighton and Regnery have written the authoritative desktop reference for marketing managers to be consulted before saying, "O.K. Let's go with it." Included are the most up-to-date changes and hundreds of clear answers to the full range of marketing and advertising questions from sweepstakes, discounts, competitive pricing, prizes to multi-level pricing, dry testing, unordered merchandise, warranties, lists, debts, privacy, environmental issues, copyrights, trademarks, and how to deal with lawyers. Introduction by Jack Miller, President of Quill Corporation.

Hardbound, 280 pages, $70.00

WEALTH PRESERVATION AND PROTECTION FOR CLOSELY-HELD BUSINESS OWNERS (AND OTHERS)

by Jonathan G. Blattmachr

Wealth Preservation is *the* definitive book on estate and financial planning written by one of the most respected legal experts in the United States. The comprehensive information provides a rare opportunity for the reader to access professional knowledge usually limited to the exceptionally wealthy. With the recent changes in taxation and marginal rates, this is the book that tells you how to keep the government from getting everything. Written in clear, understandable language, *Wealth Preservation* is a book that you will want your lawyer, accountant, estate planner and financial advisor to read. It touches on almost every financial question that can be imagined. Jonathan G. Blattmachr is a partner with the prestigious New York law firm of Milbank, Tweed, Hadley & McCloy and advises many of the wealthiest business owners and families in the U.S. on their estate planning.

Hardbound, 650 pages, $190.00

For details write:
> Lakewood Books
> 50 South Ninth Street
> Minneapolis, MN 55402

> or call 612/333-0471